Brandin
Overcomes A Bad Day

Written by
Catherine McCauley, LPC, LSW

Illustrated by
Brandin L. Blake

AuthorHouse™
1663 Liberty Drive, Suite 200
Bloomington, IN 47403
www.authorhouse.com
Phone: 1-800-839-8640

First published by AuthorHouse   9/25/2008

ISBN: 978-1-4343-8145-3 (sc)

Printed in the United States of America
Bloomington, Indiana

This book is printed on acid-free paper.

Hi,
my name's
Brandin.
What's your
name?

I live in a little town called Sunny Buck.

I am a fourth grader at West Branch Elementary School.

I have two little sisters, Briana and Kelsey.

We live with
our mom in
a big house.
She's a nurse
at the
Sunny Buck
hospital.

Yesterday was an EXTREMELY bad day. Have you ever had a really BAD day...one of those days you thought would never end? Yesterday was one of those days for me.

It all started when mom's alarm did not BUZZ and we were late for school.

My sisters and I were rushing around the house trying to get ready. I couldn't find my favorite pair of jeans. I looked EVERYWHERE for them.

When I asked mom if she had seen them, she answered in a frustrated voice, "No, I haven't. Just wear anything. You're going to be LATE for school!" I ended up wearing a pair of jeans that were too short and too tight.

Then Briana was taking TOO much time in the bathroom, so I hollered, "Hurry up Briana!" She just yelled back at me and STILL took her time. I didn't have enough time to wash my face, comb my hair or brush my teeth. YUCK!

Unfortunately, we missed our school bus so mom had to drive us to school. In the back seat of the car, Kelsey kept making faces at me. I felt really mad, so I poked her. Kelsey yelled, "Mom, Brandin poked me!" Mom told me to leave her alone. I crossed my arms and GLARED out the window.

I was late for school. My teacher, Mrs. Lampinen, had already started our morning English lesson. As I took my seat, I felt like everyone was staring at me. How EMBARRASSING!

When it was time to turn in math homework, I realized I'd left mine at home. My stomach felt like it had KNOTS in it. I started imagining Mrs. Lampinen yelling at me and embarrassing me in front of my whole class. She didn't do that at all. Thankfully, she spoke in a calm voice and said, "Brandin, my expectations are the same for everyone. You may turn your assignment in late, BUT...points will be deducted."

At lunchtime my friend David was goofing off and spilled his milk on my already too short and too tight pants. Everyone at the table laughed hysterically. The milk felt cold and sticky. David apologized but didn't help me clean it up. I felt ANGRY.

After lunch, Mrs. Coffield, our school counselor, asked me if I was okay. I shook my head NO and said, "Not really." She gave a comforting, friendly smile and said, "If you need to talk about it, you know where to find me." So, I went to her office.

MY FEELINGS ARE ALL OK! IT'S WHAT I DO WITH THEM THAT COUNTS!

Mrs. Coffield believes our feelings and problems are important. She also thinks we can do some things to help us feel better when we feel bad. She helps students come up with solutions to their problems. I was experiencing LOTS of problems and needed some solutions. I wanted my bad day to end.

As I described my day to Mrs. Coffield, she wrote a list:

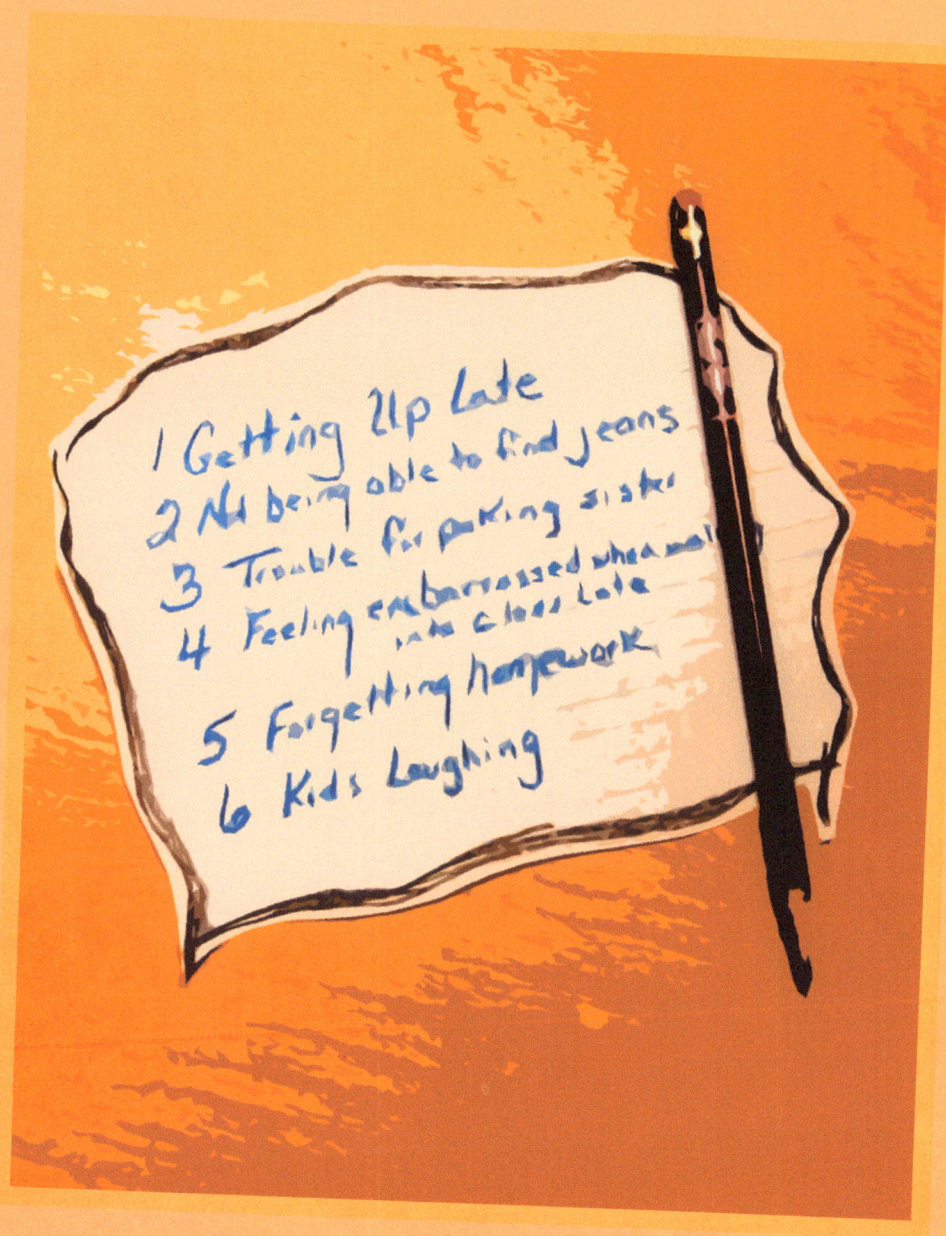

1. Getting up late
2. Not being able to find jeans
3. Getting in trouble for poking sister
4. Feeling embarrassed when walking into class late
5. Forgetting homework
6. Kids laughing at me

We worked together and came up with ideas to help me solve my problems.

I decided I can make my mornings smoother and less stressful by setting out my clothes before I go to bed. I can also make sure everything I need for school the next day is in my backpack. AND... it probably wouldn't hurt if I cleaned my room.

Instead of getting mad when my sisters are being so annoying, Mrs. Coffield suggested complimenting them. I wasn't sure I could do that. So we practiced something I can say when Kelsey makes faces at me. I came up with, "Wow, you look cool even when making faces." That will catch her off-guard and hopefully she'll leave me alone.

Now I realize that when I make a mistake, like forgetting my homework, consequences will happen, but I'll get through it. I can accept responsibility without feeling so embarrassed. The important thing is that I learn from my mistakes. We ALL make them!

Last of all, we talked about what I can do when someone laughs at me. Mrs. Coffield told me a story about a time when she did something embarrassing and others laughed at her. She decided to laugh with them by making a joke about the situation. She said in my case, I could say something like, "My pants WERE a little thirsty today." We giggled. Giggling felt better than getting upset.

It felt really good to talk to someone about my BAD day and now I have some NEW ideas to try.

That evening mom made macaroni and cheese...my favorite! Mom asked how my day went. I smiled at her and told her ALL about it. She hugged me and said, "It sounds like you've learned A LOT today." I sure had.

Remember, the next time you're having a bad day you can try some of the things I learned. At the very least, you can talk to someone you trust about it. They can help you feel MUCH better.

Do you have any ideas for getting through a BAD day?

I think today's going to be a GREAT DAY in Sunny Buck!

Special Thanks to:

Blake Williams
Alyssa Girondo
Natalie Thorpe
Debbie Thorpe
Melissa Lampinen
Caitlyn Lampinen
Allison Lampinen
Katelynn Rhodes
Kelsey Rhodes
Andrew Nesselroade
David McCauley
Brandin Blake
Briana Blake
Kelsey Blake

www.ingramcontent.com/pod-product-compliance
Lightning Source LLC
Chambersburg PA
CBHW041532280526
45792CB00004B/1473